Adiabatic Flame

poems by

Shari Crane Fox

Finishing Line Press
Georgetown, Kentucky

Adiabatic Flame

For Ron, who was tough when I needed it,
Kate and Angelique,
who were kind when I needed it,
for my children, who believed, and for my husband,
who didn't run away screaming when I once said,
"Your degree is in English Literature?
Would you like to see a poem?"

Copyright © 2025 by Shari Crane Fox
ISBN 979-8-89990-107-2 First Edition
All rights reserved under International and Pan-American Copyright Conventions.
No part of this book may be reproduced in any manner whatsoever without written
permission from the publisher, except in the case of brief quotations embodied in
critical articles and reviews.

ACKNOWLEDGMENTS

Grateful acknowledgments to the following literary journals where some of
the poems, in their original form, have been published:

"Hypnopompic hallucination of you and your ex in a horse pasture five miles
outside of Greensboro," *North Carolina Literary Review*
"The neighbor lied when he said;" "Poem about the bottle blonde ex who
stole your dog;" "Sharing a drink with Death in a quiet pub on 2nd St.,"
Cathexis NW
"Adiabatic Flame;" "Loaded trunk falling down a flight of stairs like choir
birds," *Verseweavers*
"Ignore: transitive verb, to refuse to take notice of, from Latin ignorare;"
"Love Song for Dissociation," *Yellow Medicine Review*
"Desire," *Conclave*
"Fire tree and the indigenous grasses," *San Diego Poetry Annual*
"Arrhythmia," *Peninsula Poets*

Publisher: Leah Huete de Maines
Editor: Christen Kincaid
Cover Art: Barbara DuRand
Author Photo: George Fox
Cover Design: Elizabeth Maines McCleavy

Order online: www.finishinglinepress.com
also available on amazon.com

Author inquiries and mail orders:
Finishing Line Press
PO Box 1626
Georgetown, Kentucky 40324
USA

Contents

Part I

Hypnopompic hallucination of you and your ex in a horse
pasture five miles outside of Greensboro 1

On a frozen pond, ... 3

Paradigm 4

When it's bad, but not quite bad enough to leave… 5

Someday 6

He left his phone out 7

Quick-Rise Revenge Sexes 8

The neighbor lied when he said 10

The day you gave me back your ring 11

Arrhythmia 12

Part II

Adiabatic Flame 15

While I was cracking crawfish, you said you wanted to settle
down 16

Catenary 18

rush of wind through leaves 21

Desire 22

"Fire tree and the indigenous grasses 24

Ignore: transitive verb, to refuse to take notice of, from Latin
ignorare 25

Loaded trunk falling down a flight of stairs like choir birds 26

Trust 28

Poem about that bottle blonde ex who stole your dog 29

Anniversary 30

Sharing a drink with Death in a quiet pub on 2nd St. 31

Part I

Hypnopompic hallucination of you and your ex in a horse pasture five miles outside of Greensboro

You're with him again,
waiting for your scrap of connubial bliss
like a dog beneath the table,
your mind having
plopped you
into a pastoral scene this time,
tension dimpling
like the dry field grasses
scratching at your ankles.

And because it's a dream,
he's lost his paunch and his indecision,
    a typey bull of a man,
stacked
like a bulldog on a sidewalk.

You tell yourself there must have been a time
when it all meant something,
    when the distance
didn't warm you
like coffee in your favorite cup.

You tell yourself that there are cracked cup people,
    and there are new cup people, and honestly,
this isn't your first
cracked cup.
Divorce is such a delicate thing.

Still, the gardeners work the yard
because someone needs to please the neighbors.

You tell yourself there must have been a time
without excuses bleached like grass beneath
a bucket, a time without grief
cozying up behind you
with a hard-on.

You remember a spotted dog
you once rescued,
how you took her with you
to the pasture
as the sun palmed the hills,
how gently she touched her nose
    to the nose of your spotted pony
before she laid down
and died.

That pony stood guard
over the corpse all evening,
as if grief can fill any shape it is offered,
    as if a marriage,
which begins with so little,
must finally ask for everything.

On a frozen pond

On a frozen pond,
two ice-skaters glide apart.
Our empty marriage.

Paradigm

After Billy Collins

Lust is the first thing to go,
followed obediently by distain and disinterest,
the heartbreaking sophistry, the entire song of your love
becoming one you have never sung, never even heard of,

as if, one by one, the hopes you used to harbor
for a life together decided to take the keys and leave
for a small mountain town where there is no internet
aside from at the library on Tuesday afternoons
between 2 and 5 pm.

Long ago you kissed evenings cuddling on the couch
goodbye and watched tenderness pack its bag,
and even now as you celebrate your anniversary
something else is slipping away, his birthday perhaps,
his favorite cake, the beach where you first kissed.

Whatever it is that you are trying to regain
is missing from the tips of his fingers when you touch.
It has been discarded with the cancelled checks
and unused vacation.

What you seek is no longer firm between the sheets
or even streaming from a speaker,
it has hitchhiked a ride in the opposite direction
while you were asleep.

No wonder you rise in the middle of the night
and think about the boy you knew in high school.
No wonder the moon behind the clouds seems to have drifted
from a love song you once knew by heart.

When it's bad, but not quite bad enough to leave…

    What would it be like
to think of him
as just another type of aphasia.

The heart pulls its own sutures.
Isn't it like a sunset behind curtains that you draw back
to find a lamp?

It's not a friend you called when you were lonely
and it went to voicemail,
or him

after he grabs at you
crudely
before rushing out the door.
You stare at the fumes

cradling the butt of his truck.
I need to figure out why I do this to myself,
you say to no one.

Still, the heart stares in the direction of leaving.
You realize there are people who cut,

    and people who cleave
and you need to do *something*; you're tired of bleeding.
You know it's time to decide

when you find the songbird
outside your house.
Its head is tucked

beneath a still-warm body—you realize
it trusted
    a reflection
of light.

Someday

"You must change your life."
—Rainer Maria Rilke

You tell yourself someday, because someday means there is still hope,
but you know hope is on a plane to Cancun and getting drunk on
vodka and canned pineapple juice. You tell yourself someday,
because someday is a primer that will take the paint of any story. At
night, you hear moths throwing themselves at the windows. You
wonder if there is a way to feel even smaller. At night, you remember
all the reasons you told yourself to stay. You fill your own mouth
with sugar; make an oath against a stick. It doesn't help. Someday has
landed, the wheels touching down politely, like a business card
pressed against a palm. You know it won't last—someday will come
after you like old spice and chicken wire. Pretend it won't hurt if you
have to. You know what you need to do. Come here. Come close
to this poem. Closer. Listen to it. It knows you deserve better. We
both know you've outgrown someday like a piece of cheap jewelry.

He left his phone out

He left his phone out.
Autumn, his lover, texting.
The last oak leaf drops.

Quick-Rise Revenge Sexes

Pretend to be asleep when he returns home, late.
Pretend you don't notice the after-sex
  smell of his body.
Say nothing. Wait for him to leave.

Go to the kitchen
and collect your ingredients.

Lay them out in order:
  Thin Excuses-2 C
  Flaccid Fables-1/2 C
  Obvious Obscurations-2 TBSB

Sift together and pour onto a lightly floured
cutting board. Knead dough until
stiff.
When doubled in size, punch down.
Wrap in cellophane.
Store in a cool dark place.

Unwrap when completely chilled
after he returns home from another meeting,
late. Place on a cutting
board.

Select a knife sharper than his promises.
Pretend you don't notice the flush of his cheeks,
how his eyes shift to the corners of the room.

Slice. Thinly. Say nothing.
Wait for him to leave.

Place dough pieces into a pre-heated oven.
You will need to bake them three times:
  One time for when he didn't come home.
  One time for when he didn't answer your text.
  One time for when he was too tired for sex.

Set the oven timer.

Receive a call from your man.
He'll be working all night on a project. Say
nothing. Lay back.
Relax. Wait for the chime of your oven timer.
Wait, and think about your ex-boyfriend.
Think about the way his hips moved.
    Touch yourself.

Think about your ex-boyfriend
with his chest pressed against your breasts,
his hand squeezing the back of your neck.

Touch yourself harder, but don't come.

When the timer goes off, poke the dough.
If ready, the surface will be firm.

Remove your baked angers from the oven.
Lay them out on a counter.
Do you see the shiny corners, the way
they sparkle in the dark?

Bring one to your mouth.
    Feel it on your tongue.
Swallow slowly.

Pack the rest in a basket.
Cover, they are best when served warm.

Get dressed. Hurry—
your ex-boyfriend is probably hungry.

The neighbor lied when he said

> he saw my legs around
another man's neck through the kitchen window.

I'm a good wife. I was only late for a lunch meeting.
> The raspberry

thing he saw was simply a candle
melting slowly, the wax sliding between my thighs.

I'm sorry he lied, I am not that kind of girl.
I'm afraid of heights

> and spiders. I have delicate fingers.
I'm the girl next door, a picnic on a Sunday afternoon,
saltines and warm tomato soup.

> I'd never
be a Manhattan skewered by a sodden cherry,
> or a cherry at all,

> and *certainly not* an olive with that red thing
> pushed into the center.
No, I'm sensible sweater and patent leather.

Besides, how could there be someone else?
Isn't love forever?

The day you gave me back your ring

I was sitting on the porch
and at first

I didn't see you, what with
the exit sign

pointed at your head.
You were trying

to ignore it all.
You were like a shadow

beneath an abandoned car, your
mouth bleeding into the

street. Please don't worry.
This is not as bad as it

sounds. You placed your
ring on the porch near my feet.

I dropped it
into a potted plant.

Just past our porch,
a phone pole wore its usual

protests. Above us,
a prop airplane moaned.

In the distance,
someone who looked a lot like you

stood at the edge of a tall building,
a house on his chest.

Arrhythmia

Because it is easier to lose something
after you name it, or because the heart,
like a diamond, grows
hard under pressure: a lick of oil,
your tongue to my palm,
the warm nights I waited for you to
tell me goodbye,

because my anxiety cannot tell the difference
between a fight and a visit,
or the circular motion of blood from the secrets
I wish I could tell you,
like the heart is the size of a fist,
or the heart has fronds
that sling it together,

because the heart, like the two of us,
is built to fly apart,
and because the heart only breathes
what the body discards,
and isn't it ironic that the faithful heart can only
feed itself between
beats, and it isn't lost on me
how easy it is to forget
a regular rhythm,
so isn't it fitting that the heart, when
injured, sings to itself?

Part II

Adiabatic Flame

I chose to say it,
knowing it wasn't
the right salve to sooth the bruise
blooming in your chest: but still;
some sharp part of me
loves the taste
of blood beneath my tongue. I'm sorry.
If you call again, I won't answer.

A ruby throated hummingbird
hesitates above; pollen comes down.
I wound you where I'm wounded;
that bruise keeps its color. I'm the mess
left after the blue heron lifts off
from the pond; the unwanted troth;
an empty palm.

I'm sorry. If you call again, I won't answer.
You'll just say (again) that I'm afraid
to commit; I won't say you're right.
In my mind, you're a snare, an abyss. Truth,
a bloom in the fractured mind,
has no part in this.

While I was cracking crawfish, you said you wanted to settle down

Other friends have flown before
      —Edgar Allan Poe

I said nothing.
Time has a way of circling, a way of

dropping things.
What would I do

with what is left of me
after you?

This is not white snakes or thunder,
this is me wondering

if you are oneiric or a cliff.
What if I'm your river ghost. No,

that's not it,
I'm a winter fox

running along cold water pressed slow
by ice,

images of you
caught in my mouth.

You said you wanted to settle down.
I stared at the gumbo.

Let me pretend it will be you
getting drunk with me in New Orleans

three years from now.
Let me pretend you true.

Settle down?
I'm afraid you can't mean it. What if

crows are already flying
above the bijoux.

What if I've already smashed
every clock that

told time
without you.

Catenary

After Jane Hirshfield

Dating again. It feels so vulnerable,
like a letter you don't want to open.

But the days arrive, even when they aren't invited,
like today, with you
in this quiet café with its patio
rimmed in dense purple flowers.

There are times you knock today
up against the past
to see what breaks. If you're brave.

Which I'm not.
I'm telling you about my neighbor's cat.
It's a safe subject—
my anxiety likes it.
You lean forward, the cruel years
at the tips of your elbows.

You see, my neighbor's fat orange cat
keeps shoving himself
beneath the fence.
He wants to romance my tabby. But she's ancient.

Spayed.
She wants none of it.
Still, he persists.

If I chase him from the back yard, he runs to the front.
It might be the only time he runs.
Why does he keep trying?
Why her?

And why am I sitting here with *you*,
someone I dated in high school
until another girl you dated

cornered me
and I won't say those bruises were fun,
but aren't some equations solved
by separating variables?

It doesn't matter.
It was only high school.
Justice was off somewhere reading the history of nothing.

It was only high school. Did I say that?
We were learning about life
and anxiety and the ways people lie,
and now it's been
    years
and you're divorced
and still gorgeous
and back
like that damn orange cat.

Meaning, why me?
Meaning, maybe I should leave. Meaning, trust me, I'm only good
at endings.

Please, you tell me, *please stay for something sweet.*
You're like that orange cat. I can't.

   It's one of those minutes that takes hours.
   I stare at my hands. Beneath the table, sandals.

Breathe, you tell me, *it's only dessert.*
I hum.

Outside this small café,
gulls screech against the windows,
red lights change.

You've ordered a tart, garnished with sugared orange rind.
Two forks.

You're crying.
The tart is adorned
with a salt & pepper diamond.

rush of wind through leaves

rush of wind through leaves
a crane lifts off from the lake
words I should have said

Desire

This afternoon, I watched a crow drop
a nut and crack it on the hot asphalt.
Some cars whizzed past and one of them

ran over a portion of the bird's wing.
It flapped its one good wing and began to
hop away, leaving the nut, as another car

whizzed past and ran over its tail, while the
first car made a u-turn and came back around,
this time aiming for the other wing and

pinning it to the pavement, as the second car
honked and made a u-turn and waved a hand
out the window to the first car, a thumb's up

gesture. This didn't really happen, but I'm
running out of ways to describe what is supposed
to be this glorious thing called love. You see,

my lover is having another woman over to his
home tonight. He's poured wine and made her
dinner, pasta he says, just the two of them, and

she's just a friend, he says, and she's single, but I
only know this because I asked. I'll start over.
This evening, I went to the grocery store and

there was a mother who asked her daughter to
pick out a head of lettuce, but each time her
daughter tried to put the lettuce into the basket,

the mother said "No, not this one." This went on
for seven or maybe ten heads of lettuce, before
the mother said she was no longer in the mood

for salad. Let me try again. Tonight, I should
be leaving you, but I'm waiting by my phone
the way a solitary dog waits by the front door.

"Fire tree and the indigenous grasses

After Wislawa Szymborska

Love is the one
way to fall face-first into everything,
to run a black diamond slope
like you fell from a tree at fourteen;

to be a sunbeam
cracked apart
as you pass through a windshield;

to tell a fuck
from everything that it's not;

to cut a path through the grass
of your own life or dawdle like a lap dance;
to remember, for a moment,
a choice that changed everything;

and if only once, to light the body's fire
into twist-tight blue mercury
so that when your lover calls,
you'll leave your work in the den;

become an autumn tree
flinging leaves, skin that only touches
itself; or something you try once with
your lover, but never again."

Ignore: transitive verb, to refuse to take notice of, from Latin
ignorare

And this is how we loved: our palms
pressed together, petals of spring beneath our feet,
and then,

December and your beard
turned cold with ice, the long phone calls
and your hand in the dark.

And this is how we shattered: A fifth of 4 Roses Whiskey
the afternoon after your mother's funeral, your hands
sliding beneath my waistband, my pants rumpled on the floor.

The sound of your grief covered our ears until we could not
hear the sound of your past, your father sliding
into your room in the dark,

his selfish puncture of your childhood,
and your mother, a proper teacher, for years,
pretending she did not know.

Loaded trunk falling down a flight of stairs like choir birds

If you must know something,
know that all I remember of our first date
was the fifth of big bottom whiskey. Know

that there are things from your past that don't belong
in your presence.
That a bruise is where a childhood should be.

That the man
I saw through the window was only light

rubbing up against a coffee shop pane—
                        no matter how bright his hands.
While I slept, he sold his last Lalique to buy my ring.
He lay behind me
and placed his past against the curve of my spine
                        where it melted into knives.

Crows climbed across the sky. Below, rust. & more rust.

We had been burning memories, ash in our mouths. Decades
like machetes. Like hips. Or any instrument of torture.
                        He leans over. Tips my chin.

We were running for years—
the edge of our fear nowhere in sight.
When we left Portland, the carcass was still warm.
Otherwise, it was a beautiful

wedding. Pale orchids dying on our shoulders.
The water Riesling blue
as the turtles went on swallowing bright pieces of plastic.

Sea weed. Used drink straws. A condom turning in the surf.
He said, *The sound of fighter jets*
is like God turning up the reverb. He said,

There is something about me you should know. It sounded like *gun,*
like *father.*

He invited me to his parents' house.
I use the word *house* here, in lieu of *home.*

He invited me in. Grand piano. Silver.
His mother was in the kitchen looking up the meaning of mercy.

Trust

After "Yellow," by Mary Oliver

There is the heaven we enter
through institutional grace,
and there is the way you sigh in your sleep
when I lay my arm across your body
in the tight fist of the night.

Poem about that bottle blonde ex who stole your dog

After Adrian C. Louis

Somewhere
someone
who now is
no one
to you with
her long gone
& us wed
is lifting her
ghost head
I found your
pieces after she
made you
her factotum after
she stole your
schnauzer
your money your
best whiskey
and left you
like an old couch
& she is nothing
to you now
but very much
present again today
on AirBnB of all
places you got
20 dollars off
because she went
somewhere
but not where
I'd like to send her

Anniversary

All I know is
the taste of
purple when the sun
sets warm
    against our deck.
Later, the breeze.

You can almost
see it—
like the first time
    someone you love
leaves you.

There are different
    kinds of
broken, and I am as
lost as you,

but it's dusk, darling.
The pines are dressed
in purple
    and your breath
is soft against my neck as the
last crow
    cuts the sky.

Sharing a drink with Death in a quiet pub on 2nd St.

I'm working on a poem
in a red leather booth during happy hour

when Death walks in. Perky breasts. Miu Miu flats
and the legs to match.

She sits down across from me, uninvited. She smiles.
That makes one of us.

This is my writing time.

Trying to be polite, I tell her
    The things I don't have time for are the things I want most.

Death agrees.
She orders me a drink.

Nice wedding ring, she says,
tracing a nail across the back of my hand.
    Thank you, I reply, *it's new.*

She leans forward, cleavage winking.
Taking a bride, she tells me,
is one of the worst

parts of my job. I prefer the elderly,
or people in pain who are happy to see me.
But to take newlyweds, newborns,

or someone with a new puppy? These are the jobs I save
for the end of the day...
—if I don't call in sick.
She downs her Bloody Mary.

I show her my poem. She agrees it needs
another stanza.

We order one
more
round.

Shari Crane Fox is a physician and Best of the Net Poetry Nominee. She holds advanced degrees from Mayo Clinic, Stanford, UA, and UCSD. Her poetry has received the Margo LaGuttuta Award, Florence Gibbs Award, Arizona State Poetry Society Award, Mass State Poetry Society Award, Power of Women Award, Ohio Award, and Carl Sennhenn Award, among others. She is a double board-certified psychiatrist who practices in Del Mar, California on unceded Kumeyaay land. She especially enjoys working collaboratively with creatives, diverse individuals and children, executives and medical professionals, and those who feel stuck, stymied, stalled or burned out. If you catch her in a weak moment, she might admit to surviving internship at Stanford by secretly writing poetry during rounds. She resides with her partner and an assortment of rescue beasts, and enjoys kayaking, baking, and a good pour-over.

www.ingramcontent.com/pod-product-compliance
Lightning Source LLC
Chambersburg PA
CBHW020223090426
42734CB00008B/1192